Reservations

Reservations

POEMS BY

JAMES E. RICHARDSON

PRINCETON UNIVERSITY PRESS

PRINCETON, NEW JERSEY

Copyright © 1977 by Princeton University Press
Published by Princeton University Press, Princeton, New Jersey
In the United Kingdom: Princeton University Press, Guildford, Surrey

All Rights Reserved

Library of Congress Cataloging in Publication Data will
be found on the last printed page of this book

Publication of this book has been aided by a grant from the
Paul Mellon Fund of Princeton University Press

This book has been composed in Linotype Granjon

Printed in the United States of America
by Princeton University Press, Princeton, New Jersey

for John

ACKNOWLEDGMENTS

The following poems have been published previously:

"A Few Things for the End" in *aspen leaves*

"Instructions for a Commando" in *Carleton Miscellany*

"Sieges" and "The Will" in *Concerning Poetry*

"Encyclopedia of the Stones" (section 45, as "Possibilities") in the *New American Review*

"An Age," "In the Museum of the River," and "The Tracks" in *Padan Aram*

"Driver Education," "Ransom Note," and "A Season of Farewell" in *Poetry Northwest*

"Somebody Else" in *Prairie Schooner*

"The Condemned" and "The Crime" in *Shenandoah*

"Encyclopedia of the Stones" (except section 45) and "Homing" in the *Virginia Quarterly Review*

"A Coast" (as "Dimensions") and "The Vanished" in the *Yale Review*

CONTENTS

Reservations

In Touch

When for no reasons but his own the silent cat
throttled your song,
I buried you in the tone-deaf garden,
alone, as I thought.

But when the shimmering catch
of sun unrolled—
blazon of corn, flourish
of feathery fennel,
deep liquid melon trill—
you are up,
and holding level in the level air
inconceivable wings!

At the first defeat,
the unutterable concentrations, the bullet grace,
disband.
The blood darkens, the eyes crowd,
the body like a vast party breaks up
into smaller and more passionate nights.

Bird, bright metal, renegade nerve, whom
no one ever touched, you now
touch openly,
and in the long and careless sun
unfold and loll and glow.

Far far down everywhere,
where even the light is far apart, the very eye
invisibly huge, matter waits in endless lines
to find out what it is.
Into the mindlessly small
the mind may not enter; nor touch
into the untouchable.

So we are just passing through
each other, deep embraces like a bullet's
kiss and ricochet; or say
we hold as waves
seize, hold, O never hold, the shore.

The willing, nervous living flash and fly.
The stubborn dead relent, and die. And die
into us, craggy water that our memories
labor to admit. They are ours

when they are not their own.
They walk into the grave, and do not stop,
but break, join hands, and breed
with stone, and slug, and light, and dandelion.

The Tracks

They come every night,
those cavernous trains, tornadoing
the frozen house,
a madness feeling for the door.

And it is hard even to imagine
the neighbors in a bath of light
playing small cards,
their windows in precipitous lines

downhill to where the silence leans
like blocks of onyx quarried
from the white moon,
tomorrow already in ruins.

So I arrange some little miracles—
the walls do not dissolve, the kettle
shrieks tea—
and pick across the hours as though they were

loose stones in a stream.
December, and again under the wheels
of stars,
of chances out of hand, and of the rage

careening mountain-long, I bend
and am nighted by necessity.
For though it all
seems unconnected, who can tell

what he has chosen to forget
by simply standing on line.
Maybe that
the far hand already bleeds, a bridge

has bowed, a tie has broken. That on the spur
of this moment, the tracks, the
labyrinthine nerves,
tense and gleam, hurrying the news.

Elegy for a Cousin

Even as a child you were the worst
at hide and seek. Everything pointed to you,
highlighted in August on the axle
of the formal garden, saying *This is the hardest.*

But at six on the terrace, the flagstones
breathing back heat, the rusty plaint
of the swinging couch indistinguishable
from crickets, you were not beneath your silence.

Dismissing your losses, you called for the game—
found again, rapt on the doorstep, feet
listening in the ivy, obvious on the walk,
saying *Yes, but how did I get here?*

Why in the stuttering firelight did you gaze
on the deft needle diving and gleaming up
through the falls and pools of silk, saying
No one is followed, why did you wake,

some days, before us all to circle
the house, touch all the bases, slide between
meticulous split rails, pick through the rock
garden, saying, at breakfast, *It is not over?*

Well you have won at last. Today, drawn in
to your plot, we thread the white gate, the two
slim pines, following the trail you laid,
though we are not sure who has died.

Writing to You after Sunset

Of the rocker washed up
from the wreck of a fortune, of the softwood
porch winded and grayed down, of the ocean
doing as ocean usually does,
I say nothing. You know these
as well as I. Perhaps I should remind you
of the darkening along the page. I am
having a hard time. It is further. But you
remember.

The Vanished

When the gifted lamps descended on your sleep,
it was one wish you never thought to rub up;

so you stuffed your shameful baggage to the brim
and trundled southward in the wake

of murderers, embezzlers, and the retiring
sun. Fifty miles. Now you're true!

You, not asking, got what silence calls—
the redeeming genius for being forgotten.

Those timid letters home drew no demands
for what you had. (Who wanted

that?) You fill the former home
of someone. No one wonders any more

(not even you) about your face, the holes
in your story, or where you get what you live on.

A Season of Farewell

All down the night the fires of ourselves
fell dim. I wake too late
to the clang and bone-crack of a thundering freeze
driving in, alone. And bury all good through the length
of the homely, hard-rutted road.

I know the half-mowed field
and the lights that scurry from the tall
cold to the unmade hay,
and lie in, safe as blades,
when the wind whets the thin moon.

Now is the meager reign
of stars. I cleave to them as skin
to winter steel. They turn inexorable
diamond-pointed wheels
on sight, the upturned stone.

And you, intractably deep-hearted one,
love, I will see far
on the road to the fire,
till you drag in, ruined, hating me,
and, disgraced, I take to you again.

Lepidoptera

When the small one graced your shoulder,
and stayed;
and stayed, as we circumnavigated the lake,
there seemed
no gravity—if this rare flake of air and gleam
could weigh so heavily, then massive us
might well fall up the blue
towering on blue.

Out of a sky that is too bright to see
mercurial visions splash in an eye,
multiplied. This is the brain
of a butterfly.

They sail,
billowing galleons;
they breathe
the lovely fire;
they dream
the leafy moon.

And stayed, but when an oar
stirred silt, became the wind,
the loss of weight no more
than something forgotten. I saw why we call
that mountainous vertigo *butterflies*,
and how we are used by such small things.

Settlements

Your house has fallen from my eye
like a tool dropped at the cry of war,
at the hand of snow. I turn my coat
to find what I can trade for life.

The sunward road's in bloom
with bones of the wind.
When the evil bears too hard
they rise and blaze and blow.

The ice puts down its feet,
crazed with the strength beneath,
and bright. The stone sets in
on its deep, disastrous journey.

The Encyclopedia of the Stones: A Pastoral
for Samuel H. Monk

1

They do not believe in the transmigration of souls.
They say that bodies move
as leaves through light.

Everything would be perfect if the atoms
were the right shape and did not fall down.

2

They resent being inscribed,
as if they could not remember;
but they congratulate us on the wisdom
of using them to mark graves.

3

Sand makes them nervous.

4

They perceive the cosmos as the interior
of a mighty stone.
At night this is perfectly clear.

5

Long ago
they began to give of their light
to build what we now call the moon.
It was almost finished.

6

Tradition says they were the paperweights of a lord
whose messages rotted beneath them.
So they think hard.

The old remember being flowers,
but the young ridicule them and remember fire.

7

Some say they were prayers
until they lost confidence;
others, the ashes
of the shrieking cold.

8

This is their heroic myth:
One afternoon the great stone set out.

It is not over.

9

They are unable to perceive moths.

10

They have a dream, but it is taking
all of them all time
to imagine it.

11

It is the same with their dance,
which has gone on since the beginning
without the repetition of a step.

12

They have computed the human life span
to the nearest hundred years.

13

Knowing them to be fond of games, I asked
why they did not arrange themselves
according to the constellations, but they said

Look.

14

Under water they hear each other
and glow.

15

On the sea floor under ungodly pressure
they harbor the sonorous drought of a day
no living thing is left to remember.

16

They are fond of each season in its turn,
regretting only brevity.

They suspect this world was not made for them.

17

No hand is slow enough, really,
to catch a stone:
the long forest burns
and grows and burns before the jostled stone
like roiled water settles clear again
to its root and its prayer and its home.

18
They recognize everything.

19
They suppose that if they could forget enough
they would become stars.

20
One of them is counting the days,
but they go so fast he cannot stop
to tell us how many.

21
Stone (stōn), noun. Originally a verb meaning
to illumine blackness, later
to hold without touching, or
to be capable of all things. In modern,
and less felicitous, speeches,
Indo-European, for example, *to thicken or compress.*
Still later, as we know.

22
Here is another of their stories:
One stone.
Like the others it is characterized
by control of plot and fidelity to the real.

23

The progress of the stone:

Primevally—a sun unto itself.
In the next age—a bend in moonlight.
Failing this—a cauldron of teeth.
Still later, pitted and harried—a dawn of iron.
In time, our time, a recalcitrant image
in a bed away from the dream.

24

They are experimenting with sex
but are still waiting for the first ones to finish.

25

They are attracted by bright lights
(especially white and blue)
at the rate of one inch per millennium.

They have large and obscure purposes
expressed as continental drift.

26

Fossils: monuments
to their tolerance. Eons
upon eons of surrender
bring a flower to bed with stone.

There is another theory: one stone
remembers one thing—
vividly.

27

They have rings
like trees, a kind of consummation,
growing from inside almost as fast
as they are eroded,
and accomplished in silence with unspeakable pain.

28

When it is unbearably clear,
the stones have taken a deep breath.

29

They have much to teach us
of what we should already know.

30

They place a high value on wit
and refuse to believe it is because they are afraid.

31

They think they eat,
but because they have never been hungry
the question is purely academic.

32

They grumble at the consequences
of leaving no stone unturned.

33

They are fond of the phrase *after all*.

34

They never had much use for birds
even before the crisis.

35

When I describe to them how we see a shooting star,
they say *That is how you look to us.*

When I tell them how they look to me,
they are elated and describe in turn
something I have never seen and do not understand.

36

Another day dawns and the stones
labor incessantly until they have
filled it with darkness.

37

Some of their favorites: October,
salt, flowers, 10 P.M., starfish,
Paul Klee, stories, waiting, the moon.

38

You know that the sky is blue
from the accumulated breath of stones,
or will, the next time you are asked.

39

When they stare at themselves too long
they become diamonds.

40

Sometimes in the intense light
they are seen to quake.
And they say *Never mind,
sun, old burrower
into our dreams.*

41

They do not understand the difference
between dying and just going away.
When I walk home they weep,
but not for long.

42

They have been called the eyes
of the lost angels,
and it is true they remember
great lights, and a fall,
and that they seem to be waiting
for something to go away.

43

Here is another one of their stories:
One day the great stone went out
and never returned.

They do not understand this one,
and it is therefore of dubious authenticity.

44

They are very clever at imitation.

45

The stones will not admit
that they are the fastest—

they would rather deceive us
than win.

Now you know what you will be
when you have forgotten everything
you need to.

Their wings are approaching:
the speck of a tern on the horizon, the wings
of an embryo,

but the darkness
will not support them, and the light
astonishes.

So the stones are waiting for another world.

Mostly they let themselves be used,
knowing they will inherit
what they become.

Some turn inside out. Those are the flowers,
dying before us.

46

They question the parable of Perseus and Medusa,
saying that mirrors, of all things,
would be no help.

47

They cannot tell the living from the dead.
Be careful to clarify your position.

48

The stones see only our feet.
They say nothing
has changed.

Yes,
nothing
certainly has changed.

It was winter when they died.
It is winter now.
That is the difference.

49

The success of unbearable intimacy: two stones,
the one to the windward finally
the more smooth.

50

I told them my favorite story:
One day.

They liked it except for the
surprise ending.

51

They know the infinitesimal ways
to the center of peach and oyster,
cherry, brain and heart.

52

They are continually astonished
at the thousands of ways we have invented
to say *I am dying.*

53

They do not mind lying in the sun,
especially when there is no choice.

54

They call themselves the abbreviation
of distance.

55

They have a proverb: *Absurdity
is marvelous, but you get hungry an hour later.*

I reply *But that is what it is for.*

56

Knowing and unknowing never love,
but form the maelstrom within the stone.

57

They have something they will say to us,
but they are revising and revising.

58

They think of the whole day
as sunset.

59

The stones are putting out their fires.
You no longer see
as many.

Only the other night is coming,
so there is no sense in burning.

The watchmen are climbing toward us like the throats
of caves
with the news so old it has never
seen us,

and the animals flee before it
into the future.

60

Along the margin of the lake,
stones in a simple line, taking account
of the shouts of generations of lilies,
are polishing the desperate poverty of life
into an opulence beyond all conception of light.

61

This whole encyclopedia reminds me of a stone.
It does not remind them of anything.

When they say *That reminds me of a stone,*
it means they will not
say anything else for a long time.

62

I asked *How can we keep you out of the fields?*
They said *Give us a place of our own.*

This was not like them.

63

They are never disappointed
because they expect nothing.

64

It is possible they would die for us
if they could find a reason.

65

They try to forget,
but their sadness for the flowers will be told
again and again,
though it seems I am no longer the one.

66

I say *How do you get to the river?*
They say *It will come.*

The Morning After

I leave my pain
locked, unlit,
and drift along the hill
to find out what is over.

For I have read that overnight
The End has thrown its glacier
off, and shrieked upon us,
as if we never knew it was there.

And now are reported an air
of lions, beacons
from the mildest stones, whole herds
of fountains; not the first

I have not seen.
Though they must be happening,
happening,
and it is strange how we survive.

For Deucalion and Pyrrha

First you were ashamed, and then you did it just for luck,
throwing the stones you'd trod on up
till then. So rose the roses—us,

flowery, rocky, wet,
branching to forget
how things fit together.

A dream of too much flesh,
stupider than death, and feeling
worse about it, we survived

never being able to imagine
what we would kill,
and with what, and without remorse.

So it is true we are the stones,
looking for something to endure.

The Dead

There is still the smell of them,
bitterer than they were, like snuffed candles,
and the skins of cold they shed
tremble between the stars.

Everywhere the imprint of their eyes! The path
turns with them. Their gestures return,
subdued, an Indian summer.
I bring a few flowers.

Why ask what is to be loved,
now there is nothing.
The question is who am I
who still walk with them.

Homing

Weren't we supposed to be
eating, growing
fat for something cold?

I forget. The leaves
wink by, traffic lights.
It is the time when no one can go,

or stop
dying, ice jam
of the heart.

Indiana! God!
What are the rules
here, of cold?

Once Paumanok,
when the snow was in bloom . . .
the Indians there

never saw it fish-shaped, straining
yearly seaward,
but knew anyway. They,

when the time came to be beaten,
saw that the situation did not entail
evacuation to the mainland, but

squeezed eastward
until their generous imaginations
conceived them birds.

And near the mouth of the Sound,
they rode their sentence out,
not pursuing

but waiting,
where the sun would sometime
thaw their cries.

And you—your hair
is growing. Are we
beasts yet? Not?

It is the archer's month!
He sees!
What fish

in air, what animal,
burrowless,
ever survived a winter?

For October

On the thirty-first of your allotted days,
you wound along the ridge dividing
the poor from the hopeful, wading high
in the last gasp of tangled undergrowth.

You plowed down the slope, struggled
up over the crest, stumbled again into sight,
taking nothing, seeing no one, as if
disappearance were your only purpose.

No one knew you were anything
but the meter reader, jiggling doorknobs,
frightening the darkness of basements
with your heavy flash, noting carefully

what we had used, what left behind.
But I saw you record the stillness
of cats shining in the high grass like streams,
praise the infinite readiness

of weeds, savor the rumble of
imminent frost. I saw you say good-bye,
good-bye to the homes, as if they were
rows of squat, tenacious greens

you had helped to plant. You with the tang
of smoke and windfalls, you
quietly revealing after the months
in disguise, before the months

in the guise of honesty. Everyone
likes you, but you need no help to
be what you are. You our best moment,
you of the grave and terrible children.

Summer kept loving us. We tried
to give ourselves away. Now we wheel,
fling off desire, bearing down
like the wind under the door.

Later, what we still need
finds us. Someone looks at a watch. It's dark.
Taking the shortcut, you outrun destruction,
not having, now, to be careful of the gardens.

Set

Long evening, thistle seed
loafing earthward.

There was nowhere to go, so we went
after driftwood, whatever

had its fill of the sea. The sun looked
further and further into the waves. The wind

rose to follow,
yawing and blundering in its sleep.

The distant flap of canvas, or the heart
climbing? Any old sail. . . .

The needles' eyes
yawn open like smoke rings.

If I wanted, if I wanted,
I could thread them, with a friend.

Elegy for the Left Hand

At birth it was still holding on. Later,
with visions of its own, it did not care to seize
the brilliant, dangling, clamorous gifts
that could not want it. Called weaker, it endured
the posturing of its twin, disinheritance,
the odious comparisons of mirrors—
bore, instead, the rings and watches, knowing time
to be safe with it. When the airy right
prestidigitated, skywrote, no one saw
the obscure weavings in the safety of pockets,
the slightly impatient tappings,
the vaguely sinister reluctance.
Parting unshaken, granted, like the condemned,
an occasional cigarette, it waited,
eternal underdog, for the fall.
Brother, left-handed from the start, you seemed
to reach away from us until you went
on ahead. Now your strong hand swings
around to us, and while the usurper
moulders, you stir in your element,
manhandling our days, helping, giving laws.

Instructions for a Commando

Paint everything black. Your knife,
strop on the long nerve (enclosed).
Repeat three times the invocation
of silence, that the thin peal
of escaping life may not betray you.
Consider each step as the last
rung on the ladder to hell. Bring
no food, no light, no
ambitions. If fires break out
in you, cover them, pressing the afflicted part
to the earth. When you must,
scream as the dog or stone.
So when they come to find something
at least it will not be you.

Plowing Under

Once you were everything. Now you are
someone I know, a spring
garishly overgrown, a lolling, excruciating lover

bent on—what? Undone in
every limb, you sag to
specificity, the eventual fire of whim.

And guess through that ungraduated marsh
the one hard way. Or is it
only yours? Floundering

behind you, who could say; but we have
lost and found.
This is the last. . . .

Is there no law but the right
of salvage? The calls omnipotent, the directions
amazed, I

save what is saved.

A Coast

Two and a half inches
behind the left eye, and receding,
there is a small hole.
It is what you are always trying to think of,
even when for a long time it has not occurred to you
that there is something.
It seems the pupil
of another eye, sometimes,
when it is dark.
When it is lighter, when it is
rocking, it is the sky,
or at least a sky
indistinguishable from the sea;
or the wind
rising with its hands full.
The sun is there, too,
but it would be hard to say
which one. A beach
on which there is no one sweeps
around behind you, and a gull has been there.

A Few Things for the End

Whatever I had the streams
long ago bore away, and the sun
rarefied or unwound,
and the growing silence each year lifted
higher for the scattering wind. Bone, and salt,
and subsidence of heart,
I bring to my last right: to be
the language of the stars, the utter stillness
that can only be seen from years away.

The Lake

A heart's length above the high-water mark,
trees begin, leaning away. Clear streams
back in. There are no visible
outlets, except the sky, and this
only at sundown when the lake
chills in its socket with reflected bitterness.
Some men come here, and dream
small, throbbing, eye-sized dreams
that will not break. The fires, too,
are small, but they are superfluous.
There are no currents, though bones
spiral from the shore. The zodiac
spins in the surface red red red. . .

A Ransom Note

Do not call
anyone, for who deserves
to be believed, and haven't you,
since the roads one October blazed and
fell from their destinations, been trying to explain
what was taken from you? No, do not
call.

Do not
try to deceive us. Valises
angular with gems, bricks of unmarked bills,
will never do. What it hurts
to give is our demand—
what no one wants but you,
who least of all believe
in your own pernicious counterfeit of pain.

Do not take
us lightly; do not
be tempted that way, for we know
the face that almost surfaces
in your most paralytic dreams, the cause
of certain early frosts, the rising edge
in someone's voice, shadows
across innumerable lives, more darkness
than you would at first believe—
we will show you over and over how it is you.
Do not take us lightly.

Do not hurry, for in
no time, as they say, we
will have our due.
Kneeling, shred your days
in flame. Heap up,
with extravagant denial, the ransom.
Though of course it is you we have and it's over
no matter what you bring.

An End of Ends

*In the summer of 1973, a crazed Southwestern ham radio
operator triggered a massive search and rescue effort with his
imitation of a child trapped in an overturned truck with his
dead father. When the hoax was discovered, and the police
began to close in, he railed at Nixon and Agnew.*

Belly up, the truck must be,
all its delicate underthings
(if we were free)
ours without asking.

A wheel's still spinning—
hours, still creaking like the well we never saw
under the daylight, pumping out of night
dark water, stinking with depth . . .

or is that tire air, which always smells
of long-dead fish, because
(you told me this) it's walked so far
in the same black pair of shoes. Still

spinning, going where
is always here. Father,
you sleep so late. Look
for me, look, I

am never far. Do you think
I am a child? The rear-view mirror's
bright with webs, and I'm so tired
of looking for myself.

When I wanted to walk on the ceiling,
you said I was part fly,
and showed me how when hit just right
they fold their bee-lines, shrink, and die;

but slowly eat the pain, taking
their blackness on themselves, and,
stones returned to water, blaze
up. So we killed seven, though there were only five.

Fixing things. *Light! light!*
you cried.
But dust is light enough,
and has no color, and no underside.

You said that earth
plummeted and spun (I held the chair), that sun
and stars pointed the hour (I saw
your hand), that the sky

was a glowing clock, and so it is—
and an ashtray, and a stick, and a wheel,
and the mike that coils down
blink distance from my eye

so I can talk. But I have never seen
anyone listen. *In heaven there is a throne.*
Brown leatherette. Who sat there would fall down.
Unless he were a fly, with a fly's smile.

In the movie they bound us to the earth
with moistened rawhide, which the rising sun
drew taut. But who was
ever forgotten. You grow

stiff as the hour, the invisible tailor who
fits you, spinning a cocoon
of vagueness, from which one fact will emerge.
Clear. But I remember how I

woke into morning, already moving,
got ready quickly (see, I'm clean!),
and walked like a stick man through the day,
balancing something, trying not to get

my face, my organs, my
anticipation disarranged.
But I was bad. We'd never go.
I gave this slick, clean fragile self

to sleep, where it idled, until out of gas.
In the mornings sometimes I forgot
that now everything was all right,
anything was all right.

Pick-up! she yelled
at the truck. They do not call,
and never, never heal.
Why blame them? They start

already old, would have us
die with, die in, them.
They, father, I
never lied.

These are the accidents
that have wheeled onto the flats
and waited for us. We know when they occur
that we have been there before,

that for the endless instructions, this
is the final model, the ship
that is the wind's glove.
And at last we are taken.

Wrap one limb at a time. Steady me
for the long night. End me.
You did everything.
I remain.

The walls arise like laws.
This blue, humming light, this red,
must be whatever star I am
to you obsequious, sky-mouthed fathers,

bringing me gifts and deaths.
One morning this end came to me,
and it no longer mattered what I did.
But I have kept something for myself.

44

Somebody Else

The one we do not know about
had no language. When he spoke, no stones
issued from his lips, no stilts
settled in their corners, and no woman
thought she was his.

The things he took were never missed:
he adjusted the light around them,
making their absence belong.
He ate his clues
over and over.

He would do anything to stay
unremembered.
He is doing it.

Sieges

The tower strikes another noon,
strikes and goes down.

The rays of bees
bow and become dust.

Rivers have uttered themselves, the ships
ridden their dim wind through the sun,

and I alone have escaped to tell you.

The Crime

All the windows have been broken
by someone desperate to see.

And though the glittering, ruined field
now is dark,

wheels of birds return,
probing for their fallen

starlight, finding
pieces after peace.

Surely a crime has been committed. Surely,
for the victims are everywhere.

Elegy for a Deaf Mute

What you could have told us,
you seldom had the patience to write,
you all eyes, you for whom
there was never an awkward silence.
I think I know. Late, too late,
the sagging air indistinguishable
from TV haze, the clocks
having mumbled off to sleep, you turned the sound
of my Nipponese space epic
down. Poor Earth faced destruction in silence.
No one at the emergency
UN session heard the invader's
fortunate flaw: inordinate
fear of mushrooms, total failure
to master Kleenex, things
that make us proud to be human. I strained
forward for the translation—
you shook your head. Next night as we
endured each other under
towering cliffs of noise at my
habitual Bore and Grill,
you gave to some invisible dial
a counterclockwise twist.
I clicked. My beer sat down. The cataract
of chatter went up in smoke.

And I saw what the hands,
the lips, the feet, the hair—the pieces—
were doing, vanishing
and funneling up in the rapids
of silence. Hard to see

what they were waving away, tapping on,
  blowing smoke at, not at
home for. I must have been blind to have seen,
  once, some tall assurance
spearheading claims one certain way.
  See the doom! The body speaks
(O, if it does!) of what too many know.
  And whether it was
our nature, or the lowland beer, or
  what I had brought, I saw
one of those images of Judgment, screams
  in longhand, tubular
bodies braided into a long fall.
  Whither? It goes on. No
milestones in the darkness. The unstrung
  elevator holds one
note without accord.
                    Of you I know
  nothing after that night. I
don't say I have never been the same
  since. I have been the same. I see
that I have always been the same.
  I hear nothing but what
you never said. I speak only what
  you will never hear. The same.
When the wind lies down, and the silence
  turns me to the trees,
I go to you. The fields rehearsed
  in emptiness are you.
Salmon break against you. Convoys
  of headlit cars are nearing
you. No one mentions what becomes of you.
  Nothing becomes of you.
Everything comes of you. I do not know.
  I do not want to know.

Southern Railway Embankment, Charlottesville, Va.

Any foot, from the sound
of water sorting through benighted soil,
will find a river; but the theory
of railroads is that nothing moves on its own.

So to this long burial strapped with tracks
no one ever comes who does not have to go
from the wrong side of them to the vague school
whose principal virtue is that it is no one's home.

Even here we kill nothing all the way
before we see how ugly it is being only ourselves
over and over. Over and over under diesels, steel
thunderously dies, but the gentle chickweed

barely stirs from its tenacious dream.
Just when we thought it was all over,
renegade hearts blared up in the capital.
Just when the golden spike was driven,

the terminals flickered and disappeared.
Just when we have given up on the sick,
they drift again within the range of grief,
this range, where the iron grip of merely going on

persuades us that we live up to nothing.
So we praise the failures: the beer cans
huddling in nests like embers, the cheesy,
ragged photo eyed to within inches of death

just to the left of the one path over the embankment,
on which the carefully planted
note, "Smith, you asshole" is bright,
bright! Smith! Smith! Don't

say anything. Ever.
Let *us* speak: the loose chicken
kicking up the garbage, the army
of dusty cats supporting the houses,

the hopeless,
hopeless red dirt, the children
with faces like abandoned roads,
the honeysuckle in torrents down the embankment

like the wake of the inexorable life.
All of us,
proud of the little love we have earned,
falling, as we all fall, into the sun.

In the Museum of the River

Here is another family portrait,
though how it got in this forsaken city,
where the tide went out and left
nothing but wishing, I shall never know.

On the wooden bridge now
older than the river, four of us
stand closer than steps. The faces,
invisible in the wind, must be

female—that is the way of the forgotten,
no matter what they were.
It is evening, the sun
paler than a thumbnail.

The house is swollen after the rain.
I have lived there, though with
no one I know. The single death
has been tastefully excluded.

The tree whose foliage touches the earth
is wider than the house. No birds
are flying out. Ever.
And lights do not work there.

The lost caption reads: *The faces
are here, somewhere.*
Probably in the bridge, which
looks like everything. They were

swept into it. Only their surprise
remains. We are swept up. The bridge is
moving, though the river is still.
No one ever notices the end of the road.

Moving In

We did the living room in black and white
and red, so there could be no question
of expensive subtlety. The vaguely
oriental look is from the random
gifts we've gotten—once, chance; now, fate:
that's what they have; *they must* like *it*.
I hate it—when it extrudes my breath
with its fearful anaconda smoothness,
though I insist that such things cannot matter.

We're settled, at least, you sigh, because
you see those road-worn hulks of dubious
sobriety as drifters. Real drift,
odds are, is shorter starts around a
single point, the mindless intricacy
of a drugged spider. Well, there we are.

We keep on feeding on a future
nearer and less appetizing day by day,
tumbling rows of books down from the attic
(because they're colorful, disheveled, warm?)
to hide the walls. It wasn't very long ago
I would say I could do anything.
Now it's not true—or at least I've found
that anything isn't what I wanted to do.

The Operations

It is usually winter. The cold
sweeps the feet, claws to the knees.
Feeling nothing, we think we can kick
what now seem habits

and get away with it.
For no one, by definition, remembers
this anesthesia, when what cuts us up
cuts, and it is a long time

before we know what is gone.

Ashes

Into the gradual evening
we wake, having only arrived
in our half of light, where dim pines,
wind-visited, seethe and snap,
but no one calls fire.

Though there is burning, burning
of a cool but tortuous kind,
and the sky flickers, burning,
and the first drops count the leaves

like a dissolving clock, and wind
down the flue to speak,
with old ashes, of bitterness.

Of bird light turned low in the nest, the powdery
moth driven under his haven;
of us with our vast
no place to be.

And it seems that this day will go on,
parallel lines never touching,
two stones in the rain.

The Condemned

Love you have been a fire so long
I recognize you as a stranger and pass on,

looking for something else to use for a heart,
now this one stutters and sparks.

It is an old race; this is the end
of its line. Flowers become men;

men, birds; birds, flames.
Only the mirrors never change

because it is their way
to have nothing behind them.

Where are those days I had reserved,
seen only sidelong, thought to return

to, in such an hour
as this? I turn them over.

Somewhere in us among the bells
of smoke, there must be mercy for ourselves,

and music—a fire someone else can tend,
a tale for the road, the ring of men.

Close

Your death the violet,
mine the smooth stone,
seem together today—
some trick the eye
plays with such small things
seen far away.

But true enough. Should I
find the violet,
you the stone,
we close
with the blind sun, and the hard wind,
and the wreckage of the rose.

The Family of Ties

When, after their fashion, the jackets,
shirts and trousers fold up, or cling
to the lean past, or embarrass themselves
out of existence, the ties still hang around.

Listening at the backs of doors, frozen
against the walls of closets, they can
never be disowned. We seem to know
that it is useless to try to forget.

When each disguise is abandoned as hopeless,
they are the weight around our necks. Their minds,
narrow or broad, their careers, checkered
or solid, were ours, and we are dismayed

to find that they always fit. Just when we thought
we had changed, there they are, signposts
of rigidity, racks of humiliations:
the motley, waiting for each new man.

Returns

We know them, bending a little
(under their visions?). From this distance,
it seems they do not mind the snow.
But we are their misgivings.

We could go
back to meet them, smaller
against the pale sun,
past the treble of darkness at five,
the garden colliding with winter.

We know them.
But it does no good to say they were ourselves.

Driver Education

When you lose your brakes,
you must change your mind about everything.
Only what you have never noticed
will help you. Avoid, at all costs, at

one cost, the sublimity of oak,
the watchtower boulder, home,
and signs of all kinds. Above all,
do not take the easy way down.

Head for the incline formerly
steep to the point of annoyance, yet
too gentle to be impressive.
Do not let your mind wander.

When your car is a scream
swung on a long rope, and the road
lets go, aim for the low, tenacious weed,
high grass, brittle scrub—in that order.

Water will help, if it is shallow enough
not to be interesting. Get the sun
at your back. Stay away from
clouds, all large animals, friends.

When you are finally ready to stop,
all that has guided and protected you—
glass, steering wheel, struts, beams
and dials—has decided before you,

and becomes your enemy. Hold
back, cursing them
past redemption, and unafraid
of their revenge—no one does this twice.

Stop. If you can get out, do so immediately.
If the car is not burning, burn it
with your clothes inside. Change your name,
though no one will know it.

By now it is March, and you will
be tempted, but the smoke
wailing over the town of your birth
is not, not really, for you.

Elegy for Ninety-Two and Two

Long afterwards it will be called fate.
In the fog that attends revelation, a blinded jet
took this slope for home.
Ninety two are here. There is no crowd.

Where the last stares
hung before the shock
of recognition, a few
tired limbs snap downwards, wilted,

pale toward the ends. In the papers,
the transition is accomplished quietly.
No one who matters now is dead. Pain,
assuming all their names, is busy for them.

So the shy and sleepy searchers, amazed
in the outcry of dogwood, comb the trail
of metal plowing in to count
our losses. They find

reasons: baggage sprung and burned.
They find altitudes
I have never understood.
Someone else must be speaking.

On the other side of the mountain,
it is clear. The dust
straggles to the sun. Pines
straighten in the lungs,
and I can see. But nothing betrays
the older fire, except a yard
or so of crumbling stone, and the single spongy log
that the creepers have not coaxed to earth.

No one knows whether it
started here, or drove
down the valley on the wind;
whether they survived, died, or had
already gone; or who they were.

I think there were two, poor enough,
too young to be childless. Someone
had willed the place to them. If they left,
they were never happy, for they still
speak of it, voices
barely distinct, as if they sifted
through a wall. Something about
the early spring, crocus gone, daffodil going,
red soil, the light last night
on the western slope.

They left among the stones a crudely fluted
flint-glass goblet, in which
the rain seems viscous, stubborn
with light.
I think it was their promise.
Which the dark days fill
for the bright to drink.

The Will

I,
being of sound,
do hereby take this time to tell you
what is left of the dead.

All my worldly possessions I leave
to themselves.

To the wrong number,
I leave my voice still in the line
when our connection vanished.

To the millionaire whom I encountered in his
secret identity of preventer of windows, an occupation he
undertook without compensation, and to whom I gave
his only moment of happiness (when he passed
in his coach, I smiled at his door) and who cannot
remember me (he was barely a child), I leave
surprise, surprise, the whole of my fortune without
its wheel, and whatever starlight is
blown down, in the hope that he may
help my father, who died years ago.

And to you (our relationship has never been clear;
who are you and
what do you want?) I leave
it to you.

Nine Thousand Days

1/1/50–8/22/74
for my electronic calculator

Downtown the underground
parking lot is six months overdue—
labor problems, weather, lack of funds—
nothing compared to
this, which any reasonable estimate
would have placed in the early fifties,
now obsolete
when it is almost through.

For no one will drive in to crank
his two cents down, though it is open
like a hat, and I keep falling on my face.
The days discount themselves.

Whatever
the one thing is that I am told to make,
the inspector of days says *No,*
and again *No,* and leaves no clues
but the few parts he approves:
this arch of pain; the light on the face
just so, but not the face; this cloud,
nearly perfect in another place; these trees;
and the end, the end, but a little further on ...

Elegy for One Who Never Lived

You who never were,
as you glided down the hall inadvertently
connecting parlor and bedroom,
as you guided,
from the bureau that was
not next to the window, a comb
to the hair that never needed to be straightened,
the morning after nothing happened
to no one you knew, you were
already ending.

A Little Answer

Light swaying
and straightening, like reeds. It has been
everywhere. The waves
sidling up the shore are strung with it,
the shells eaten through with it.
If I bend I will spill
a great blaze.

Gulls, the cry
of nights hung out to whiten. Sand,
what of the sun has slowed. Wind,
what has already happened
remembering us. There is no such thing
as solitude, though we
are what comes of it.

On the Anniversary of Your Death

September. Kids drift back to school,
rigid and sweaty in premature
plaids and wool.

The house is settling.
Beams speak out of turn. A rudderless moth
thuds in the shade,

and you move in
with the deference of dust
to crowd this emptiest of months.

You're twenty-one. You've grown.
O stay.

Going North for the Winter

I guess we have moved on. In this city
they live forever.
I know no one but you.

When I arrived, the gnat jaws
froze to the sod. I still spoke
in the accents of your country.

The stone howls when the wind
blows across it empty.
It is the sound

of glare seizing the high
sheer panes.
The spark shakes under the avenue.

Light-headed with devastation, angry
in the onset of love,
I waver along the street blown raw

with endlessness. Everywhere the indifferent rumble!
the passionate cold! the indirection
more bodiless even than I!

Coda for October

in May they sing of October

When the field is trampled, pointing all the ways
it could have fled,
and you have counted all the dead,
and the land you knew like the back of your hand
becomes the back of your hand,
then, and only then,
O it depends.

But it is clear we shall only die
once, no matter how long we practice,
that even the most persistent
cannot be bored for long,
and that our hopelessly scattershot concentration
will save us from finding more grief than we can use.

If the past will never return, if you
have neglected the praise of stone,
you will never know. There is at most
one future to be endured. Remember,
you have other life
to give for this country. Also, it is November.

The Abandoned Tracks

Another night was left
out in the rain. Deep in the grove
all you touch will water you. Gleam

needles the gloom, moments—soul
and body—fitfully blended.
You know everything until

the incline empties you. Along the crest,
the tracks lay down hard law. A towering
blue noon quavers and burns.

The ground grows gravel. The vines
fall away from the killing,
metallic hiss of sacrifice. Here, once,

we lost the other ways to go.
But the rails are softened with the rust
of angry sunsets, quiet brutal marriage

of mania and disuse. Spiked
with shards of lives it seems
I helped to lose, they narrow

endlessly west. They made us.
No doubt they are greater than we, but
nothing is due. I steel myself and

cross them. For the future is what is
already left out. If I could hold
without holding there would be no end.

I am long in believing
that nothing is coming, longer being struck
with my own incorrigible happiness.

An Age

It is when
you have labored all winter
to prove you are content, and in

your quick, cold sleep
do not hear the rain,
that you wake

astonished in the glare
of ice, the world worn smooth
as your eye—

distinction lost, all
that rugged good
glossed over.

And you walk tight-shouldered, broken-
kneed along the shine that wants you
split like a wishbone.

Frictionless, we do not come
to much. Nothing strikes,
warms, gets stuck, parts slowly—

so you do not know where you are,
flaring off,
air mooring air.

The ice has climbed
to disembody everything. Out
on a limb, it mocks

the gutless duck four months amazed
in the high shrubs. It comes
to glare through the sockets, to wedge

the bill open, to freeze
the radial array of feathers splashed
against cold shot.

And you have come down
to peer through the narrowing hole of yourself.
O the conflagration of purity! You can

hardly see you thinning
into the white burn centimeters
above the fiery path.

It is when
you have labored all winter, called
one thing another, and all

by your own name,
that the light gets hold of the world, and shakes,
and shakes you away, and only

the love you need
gathers, colors,
steadies itself, takes strenuous root.

Library of Congress Cataloging in Publication Data

Richardson, James E   1950-
  Reservations.

  (Princeton series of contemporary poets)
  I. Title.
PS3568.I3178R4   811'.5'4   76-45908
ISBN 0-691-06329-X
ISBN 0-691-01334-9 pbk.